VIETNAM 1972:
A TIME BEST FORGOTTEN

Maj. Pete Seiler

Author's Tranquility Press
Marietta, Georgia

Copyright © 2022 by Maj. Pete Seiler

All rights reserved. No part of this publication may be reproduced, distributed or transmitted in any form or by any means, including photocopying, recording, or other electronic or mechanical methods, without the prior written permission of the publisher, except in the case of brief quotations embodied in critical reviews and certain other noncommercial uses permitted by copyright law. For permission requests, write to the publisher, addressed "Attention: Permissions Coordinator," at the address below.

Maj. Pete Seiler/Author's Tranquility Press
2706 Station Club Drive SW
Marietta, Ga/30060
www.authorstranquilitypress.com

This is a work of nonfiction.

Ordering Information:
Quantity sales. Special discounts are available on quantity purchases by corporations, associations, and others. For details, contact the "Special Sales Department" at the address above.

Vietnam 1972: A Time Best Forgotten/Maj. Pete Seiler
Paperback: 978-1-957546-27-8
eBook: 978-1-957546-28-5

PROLOUGE

Days Best Forgotten is a glimpse at several days of war I experienced 40-years ago during three combat tours while flying missions over Vietnam. In war, there are few Hollywood heroes, only scared men and women on both sides of the conflict, trying to do their job to the best of their ability under extremely difficult circumstances. Each combatant feels they are in the right and fighting for their family, their country and perhaps their God. Each participant in a war, any war, views his or her experience from a highly personal perspective. This perspective is influenced not only by the specific event(s) he or she experienced, but also by where and how they each fought. The rifleman on the ground sees his/her experience in a completely different context from that of the sailor or flier. Ground, sea and air each present their own unique challenges, weapon systems and experiences. Some fight and die bearded and dirty, while others face death shaven and clean.

Those on the 'tip of the spear' see conflict in more graphic terms than the 90% who support the conflict. Military textbooks refer to this as the 'tooth-to-tail' ratio; tooth being the ones who do the actual fighting, while tail refers to those who support the conflict. If an aging "old salt" or "grunt" proudly wears the trappings of a veteran, you may ask yourself, was he/she the tooth or the tail of that 'war dog'. Please don't get me wrong, ALL veterans deserve respect and gratitude for their contribution. However, it is usually only a small group who carry physical and emotional scars of conflict through life to their grave. To the tens, and perhaps hundreds of thousands of those I have just described, I salute and dedicate this brief moment in time. Only those of you who have been "in harm's way", will truly understanding the fear, and at times despair, felt losing comrades while facing the enemy and your own fragile mortality.

Time has dulled my memory of some aspects of the following days, so I have improvised slightly, especially with dialog. I am sure everyone has one or two days in their life that they would like to forget; mortal combat presents many such days. The following is a snap shot of two such days in my life. Except for a few first names and one or two I have substituted; the events are a reasonably accurate reflection of my **_Days Best Forgotten_**.

What is a Day?

A day! What is a day? In the English language it is a simple 3-letter word -- and not much of a word at that. However, a day can represent a myriad of experiences, good, bad, or indifferent. In definitive terms, a day is 24 hours, 1,440 minutes, or 86,400 seconds long. Most of us never think of it in these terms, however. In reality, most of our days are unremarkable, repetitious, and soon forgotten. We tend to remember only the really good or really bad ones. As time rolls on even the memorable events in our lives tend to slip into obscurity, brought back to conscious thought by someone or something that serves to stimulate recall; photos, movies, people or similar situations often do this.

According to some actuarial tables, today the average middle class American male lives approximately 76 years. That equates to approximately 27,759 days. If I am average, then at age 73 I am currently at approximately day 26,645 of my life. It is somewhat disquieting to think of our lives in these terms though! One specific day I have tried to forget for 43 years, occurred in early October 1972.

It's a sleepy Saturday afternoon in early October 2014. The leaves on the hills around Birmingham, Alabama will be changing in a few weeks from summer's monotonous green to a kaleidoscope of colors. Although a beautiful time of year in the east, it is but a brief precursor to the baron trees of winter, as nature seems to transition into stoic silence. Winter is such a contrast to the vibrancy of spring festooned with flowers, new growth and new life. The afternoon sun is struggling to pass through the windows on the front wall of the study but impeded by the tightly closed blinds.

After mowing the lawn, I am now relaxing in my study; beer in one hand and the remote in the other, watching a movie "Air America" starring Mel Gibson. I should know better than to watch war programs like this. It dredges up memories best forgotten. However, it is like passing an automobile accident; it's hard not to look.

Periodic shrieks of excitement reverberate down the hall from the den where my wife Karen, an avid Auburn football fan, is watching a close game. I have never been much of a sports fan so the study becomes my refuge whenever I need some quiet time. Although it's a small room, for me it has a cozy feel to it. On one wall a small TV is surrounded by hundreds of books filling the shelves of a rather large oak bookcase. Although I have read most of them, there are still others I plan to read someday. They are a mixture of textbooks, geopolitical books whose topics have long since been eclipsed by more recent events, history, contemporary fiction and many of the classics.

The two remaining walls have occasional pieces of memorabilia. These items represent both who I once was and, perhaps to some extent, what I wish I had become. Nature and war – they seem such a perplexing mix. Man is supposed to be the superior species, top of the food chain as it were. Yet we are such a violent species. It's hard to reflect back in time and find a period when there hasn't been armed conflict raging somewhere in the world. If memory serves me correctly only some insects and chimpanzees seem to share this warlike behavior. But I digress.

The framed pictures on one wall display pastoral scenes of beautiful natural areas and stately animals. And finally, there is the remaining wall, a war wall as it were. No, it isn't a wall loaded with military plaques, or photos of Vietnam buddies, but a wall, none the less, whose contents bring back long past events best forgotten.

The wall is a light Olive Drab color on which hang three rather large black wood and glass frames. Two of the frames contain detailed pen and ink autographed reprints of McDonald Douglas F-4 Phantoms in flight. In 1976, while a flight commander at Officers Training School, the artist's son Gary had been one of my student officers. I had provided Gary's father with several photos taken while I was in Vietnam, which he used as background research for the drawings. My stepdaughter had these drawings framed for one of my birthdays.

The two drawings flank a central frame of similar size but containing a collection of brightly colored medals and ribbons. Although I had never given these things much thought, one day Karen had run across my old and faded uniform ribbon bar carelessly tossed in a box with some old photos. Since we had only recently married, she was curious about earlier events in my life.

Without discussing it with me, she researched what each ribbon represented and purchased new replacement medals. She then had them framed in descending order of importance from the DFC (Distinguished Flying Cross), the Air Medal with 15 oak leaf clusters, various other medals, unit citations and finally foreign campaign ribbons and awards. Wrapping the rather large frame in craft paper, she presented it to me for my 65th birthday. It was a very touching gesture. Little did she realize, however, the suppressed memories and emotions these bits of metal and ribbon would evoke.

A small 8 x 10 framed photo (illustrated at the beginning of this short story) rests on the end table next to my recliner. It showed Bob, the pilot, and I standing in front of our F-4E on the ramp at Ubon Royal Thai AFB, Thailand. Ubon was flanked by the Chi and Mun Rivers which then drained into the famous, or perhaps infamous, Mekong River east of the base near Pakxe, Laos. Painted on the engine intake were two red stars. Although we were not responsible for the MiG kills those stars represented, they did capture a moment in time; victory for one pilot and presumably death for two others.

As I stare at that photo, I see a trim 33-year-old Weapon Systems Officer (WSO) standing next to Bob. I mused at the figure I once was and what I have become; a grey haired, balding man with a paunch and 50 extra pounds I plan to lose someday.

The high pitch sound of a propeller brought me back to the present and the movie which was unfolding on the TV. A small propeller aircraft was landing on a short, steeply inclined, red clay airstrip perched precariously on the top of a tree-covered mountain in the middle of the Laotian jungle. A cloud of red dust rose from the parched landing strip as the prop wash stirred up the clay surface.

As a private pilot myself, I marveled at the skill and nerve, or perhaps stupidity, attempting such a landing required. The mountain peak, red clay dust, and surrounding dense jungle all looked so familiar. "Had I seen the movie before", I asked myself. Then, like a bolt of lightning, haunting memories from the past flashed into mind. That scene had awakened long suppressed memories of several days that occurred nearly four decades earlier in Vietnam. My thoughts drifted back through time to that traumatic period.

Mission to Bat Lake

It was early October 1972, when Bob and I were having our first post-mission drink in the squadron's "hooch". It was around 4 PM and we had flown a mine-laying mission that morning against a ford just east of Bat Lake. Bat Lake, so named because of its outline as viewed from above, lay just inside Route Pack One (just north of the DMZ [Demilitarized Zone] between North and South Vietnam). The North Vietnamese trucks carrying supplies to their forces in the south frequently used the ford. They had to use fords where available since we destroyed most of the bridges. The mission had been a rather 'hairy' one because the gunner manning a 57mm AAA (Anti-Aircraft Artillery) gun protecting the crossing was a Vietnamese Daniel Boone.

Over the target, Bob rolled into a 45-degree dive angle bomb run. The gunner was under his piper (an electronically generated sighting device) and we were in his cross hairs. Whoever he was, he kept us in his sights all the way down to release altitude. Knowing he was in the target box; he was highly motivated and deadly accurate. Glowing red phosphorus-coated 57 mm shells streaked up at us, passing so close on either side of the fuselage that I felt I could reach out and touch them. Why the shells didn't have proximity fuses I will never know and for which I will be eternally grateful. With only altitude fuses, they exploded harmlessly behind us as we approached the ground.

As the patch of green jungle raced up at us at over 650 feet per second, Bob kept the piper on the target while I called off the rapidly diminishing altitude. Reaching release altitude, I called "Pickle, pickle, pickle" on the intercom. Bob pulled the trigger on the stick and with "Bombs Ripple" set on the weapons selector, all 12 mines, similar in appearance to Mark 82GP 500lb bombs, released in rapid succession. Bob immediately yanked back hard on the stick causing the aircraft shudder as it struggled under the 8 G pull to recover from the steep dive.

My G-suit instantly inflated and my helmet slipped downward on my sweat-drenched forehead. Sweat also made my face slick and my oxygen mask would also slide down on my face during heavy maneuvering. Struggling against the G force, I looked back over my left shoulder at the target and saw geysers of brown muddy water shoot skyward as the mines buried themselves in the river bottom. Clearing the trees by what seemed like only a few hundred feet, we started skyward again. On occasion, Bob had a tendency to press the attack beyond the recommended release altitude if the dive angle or sight picture wasn't quite right. Although this helped increase delivery accuracy it also decreased our margin of safety.

There were a few times when I was sure leaves and twigs passed through the engines -- but perhaps that is a bit melodramatic.

As we started our climb off the target, I felt the stick slam into my left thigh as Bob instinctively rolled the aircraft into a climbing port (left) turn to rejoin the other three aircraft orbiting above. Knowing the American's tendency to fly a left-hand pattern coming off a target, the enemy gunner had swung his gun around 180 degrees and was unloading another 5-round clip of shells in the airspace he was confident we would soon occupy.

Bob, concentrating on locating the rest of the flight orbiting above, didn't see the threat off our left wing. Seeing the shells streaking by the cockpit there was no time for discussion. I grabbed the stick and thrust it violently to the right. Bob exclaimed, "Damn" over the intercom thinking we may have been hit and the controls damaged. His rapid breathing was audible over the intercom since we nearly always stayed in "hot mike" position. "Check seven!" I exclaimed excitedly. By the time he recognized the situation we were safely out of range and I released pressure on the stick.

Neither of us said a word for a while. We were both relieved to be out of the intense flak. We leveled off at orbit altitude over the target (frequently referred to as the perch) while the other members of our flight made their bomb runs. It was almost surreal watching the other aircraft as they seemed to disappear, their camouflage blending into the jungle below.

Seconds later I saw geysers of water from the impacting mine releases and the aircraft's reappearance. Each aircraft also experienced concentrated 57mm fire but all appeared to be OK. Although I couldn't see the camouflaged gun itself, following the tracer shells back to their origin revealed its approximate location. When the shells left the barrel, their initial rapid upward velocity quickly slowed and appeared to float as they neared their apogee and detonation. The tell tail black smoke from their detonation only drifted in the wind for a few minutes then disappeared.

The sky was again clear and peaceful, as if none of the previous drama had occurred. The time over target today was measured in only brief moments of butt-clenching tension followed by a long period of peace and quiet as we returned to base. The poor rifleman below, mired in the muck and mud while having to deal with snakes, insects and the enemy, bore the worst part of warfare. For them, death was usually "up close and intensely personal". However, as fliers, we typically kept our distance; seldom witnessing the horrific personal effects of our missions.

I had a keen appreciation for the differences in our respective roles since at 18; I had also served a three-year enlistment in an Infantry regiment near Mannheim, Germany. However, I was fortunate in that my enlistment was during a brief period of peace following the Korean War.

After the last aircraft rejoined the formation, we checked each other's aircraft for hung ordnance and battle damage. This was done by flying under the wingman's aircraft with only 20 feet or so separation and visually looking for holes, fuel or hydraulic leaks, damage to the air-to-air missiles, etc. Fortunately, none of us were hit that day but not for the lack of trying by that enemy gunner. I have often wondered if he or she survived the war. Over a million Vietnamese, both North and South did not.

I had preset the base coordinates in the INS (Inertial Navigation System) so Bob centered up on the return heading and we departed the target area. Except for a high, widely scattered cirrus layer, visibility was excellent. The jungle and mountains along the western edge of this war-torn country stretched out to the horizon. Here, north of the former DMZ (Demilitarized Zone), there was little evidence of the war.

Flying over South Vietnam, however, was a different story. So many areas displayed the results of B-52 carpet-bombing missions. Long strips of denuded foliage bore witness to 108 bomb craters evenly distributed for a mile or so. Brown pock marks against a green jungle. Multiply 108 bombs per aircraft times three to six bombers per flight, each slightly offset from the other, and the destruction in the "target box" was incredible. However, unknown to us, often entire regiments of enemy soldiers survived such bombing, protected deep in tunnel complexes which honey-combed much of the country side.

Reflecting on today's mining mission of the ford, it was only later that I learned the VC would detonate the submerged mines by stringing a heavy chain between two widely separated water buffalo. They would then have the animals cross the shallow river dragging the chain along the bottom. This would cause the mines to explode harmlessly thus defeating all our high-tech delivery techniques and weapons.

The war was full of such innovations employed by this determined and persevering enemy. Americans saw the war as containing Communism while they saw it as a reunification process resulting from the political and physical division of their country following WWII.

I felt the stick between my legs shake, which meant Bob, wanted to go off oxygen for a cigarette and I should fly the plane for a while. Bob was good about giving me stick time whenever things had quieted down. Charlie, the pilot I flew with while going through F-4 training at McDill AFB, Florida occasionally gave me some stick time. Since he was also a certified flight instructor, he would sign off my flight log time as well. In country, however, I was never quite comfortable flying when the flight was tucked in tight going through the clouds during the Monsoon season. I'm sure the "hot sticks" (i.e., Thunderbirds and Blue Angels) got their kicks flying tight formation. While in tight formation, unless you were lead aircraft, you couldn't afford to take your eye off the other aircraft for a split second. To me, flying 400+ knots with only a few feet between each aircraft in heavy clouds, were tension-filled moments.

Figure: Preparing for landing

Return to Base (RTB)

The rest of the flight back to base was blissfully uneventful. Arriving back in the local area Bob grabbed the stick and gave it a shake.

"You've got it," I said releasing control.

It wasn't long before the base was in sight and we descended to 1,000 feet AGL and echeloned right in preparation for landing.

Figure: Arriving back at Ubon

Once over the runway Bob made a hard breaking turn onto the down-wind leg of the traffic pattern. Each succeeding aircraft in the flight counted six seconds before also "pitching out". This maneuver allowed each aircraft to space itself on down-wind thus minimizing landing time while providing a margin of safe separation between the plane ahead. With gear and flaps down, we made a descending left turn to final.

The runway spread out toward the town of Ubon at the far end. A brief and isolated shower must have occurred before we arrived because the runway glistened as the noonday sun reflected off its wet surface. Once the correct angle of attack was established it was just a matter of "driving" the aircraft onto the runway. In the earlier F-4 models there was no flaring the aircraft for a "grease job" (slang for smooth landing). The F-4 was designed for hard aircraft carrier landings and was equipped with a 'hook' used to catch the arresting cable.

The carrier pilot literally "drives" the aircraft onto the deck at near stall speed so he/she can catch the cable. If the aircraft approached stalling, audio warnings would sound in the headset and the rudder pedals would shake. In that event it was critical to apply full power to avoid getting behind the power curve. To me, F-4 had the glide characteristics of a rock – and not a flat rock at that! In the Air Force, however, we seldom ever used the hook and were not trained in that type of landing. However, exceptions do occur now and then.

Several weeks later we had to make a carrier style landing by dropping the hook and snagging the cable at the approach end of the runway. That event occurred when we aborted a night mission in the middle of the Monsoon season and were directed to RTB with all our ordnance.

We were heavy with fuel and 9,000 pounds of bombs. The night was pitch black with driving wind and rain. I bet the commander making that call really sweated over the decision. They certainly didn't want to rearm the entire fleet the next morning if we jettisoned the ordnance in the jungle. Furthermore, the VC would welcome a treasure-trove of unexploded bombs on the forest floor. They would cut them open and salvage the explosive core for their own home-made land mines.

Bob really earned his paycheck with that landing. After catching the cable, the hook didn't release right away and the retracting cable almost snatched us off the right side of the runway. With that experience I developed a healthy respect for the carrier jocks making a night landing, in the rain, at a 140+/- knots on a carrier's pitching deck. At least our runway was long and didn't move up and down nor roll left or right.

That same rain-soaked night, as we taxied back to the revetment, I reflected on what could have happened if the hard impact with the runway in concert with the sudden deceleration had caused one or more of the bombs to fly forward down the slippery runway. The town of Ubon was at the far end and that bomb could easily have slid all the way into town. Although I doubt it would have completely armed, it certainly wouldn't have helped American-Thai relations since we were guests on their airbase. That night all ended well but it was certainly a recipe for potential disaster.

My mind reverted back to the present with the seat bottoming thump and squeal of tires which announced our return from today's mission. Throttles back, drag chute out, flaps up, and we slowed to the far end of the runway. Swinging perpendicular to the runway Bob pushed the throttles up with the brakes applied until the chute was directly behind the aircraft. He then pulled the chute release lever and the exhaust blew the chute safely into the grass. As we taxied back to the revetments, we opened our canopies trying to get some much-needed fresh air. The air greeting us was hot, humid and filled with the noise of wining jet engines and smell of burned JP4 fuel. However, it didn't smell like a sweat drenched flight suit so I considered it a welcomed alternative.

We each cleaned up our checklists in preparation for shut down. Stopping in front of our revetment, the crew chief chocked the wheels. Then Bob shut down the engines and the crew chief hooked the heavy yellow metal ladder to the left edge of the pilot's cockpit. Seconds later he scrambled up the ladder and inserted our ejection seat safety pins. It was now safe to unstrap our harnesses and stowed our gear. With boots on the ground Bob exclaimed, "I don't know about you, but I need a stiff drink and a cigarette".

Figure: Crew bus back to operations

The crew bus, which looked more like a blue UPS truck, came to a break-squealing stop near our aircraft. We climbed in the back and took a seat on the benches along each side. The driver then progressed down the flight line picking up the other three crews of our flight. There was the usual chatter among the eight guys about the mission but nothing out of the ordinary. The bus took us to the personal equipment hut where we stowed our vests, pistols, chaps and helmets. Then it was over to the operations, intelligence and maintenance debriefing building followed by grabbing a much-needed cold beer and hotdog.

Back at my quarters I quickly got out of my flight suit and boots and took a long, cool shower. After a mission some of the guys would "sack out", others would get a volley ball game started, and yet others would head to the BX or the squadron hooch. I change into Bermuda shorts and sports shirt and headed to the hooch for a shot of my favorite tranquilizer, Jack Daniels.

The hooch was our own squadron's watering hole; a combination of recreation room and bar. Although it ran competition with the Officers Club, the guys could be both more relaxed and with fellow squadron members. Unlike the "O" Club, military rank was pretty well left at the door. Although most were captains, on a typical evening the officers inside would range from a 23-year-old 2nd Lieutenant to a 40-year-old Lt Colonel.

Situated between two long buildings that contained numerous 2-man rooms, the hooch had heavily draped windows along 3 walls and the bar along the other. It was typically dimly lit and usually reasonably cool. The bar was surprising well stocked and had about six stools for crewmembers. Elsewhere in this single large room were about 6 or 7 round tables each with four reasonably comfortable chairs. You could play darts, cards, pool, ping pong or just shoot the bull while drinking until the day's memories gratefully faded into obscurity.

We all kicked in money each month to pay for a civilian caretaker. He was a small, slim, middle-aged Thai with a family off base who maintained the recreation room and tended bar. Although I can picture him today, I can no longer remember his name. But then I can't remember the names of most of the guys in the squadron anymore. We all had a running tab that he diligently maintained in a notebook. Periodically he would hit us up for money if the tab got too high or when it was payday.

Bob was already there when I walked in. Gradually some of the other crewmembers that flew the morning mission started to wander in as well. I ordered my usual and sat down at one of the many empty tables. The ice cubes in my glass felt refreshingly cool. Although the overhead fans were running, they were only stirring rapidly warming, humid air. The air conditioner tried to keep up with the early afternoon heat but it was having trouble doing so. I took the glass and rolled its wet, cold surface across my forehead. It seemed to help the dull headache creeping over me. I thought to myself "I need to see if the guys in personal equipment can put a thinner forehead pad in my helmet. Perhaps it would help reduce these post-mission headaches." The noise level was starting to build in the room as more and more crews filtered into the hooch. Some were discussing the morning's mission while others were starting up a poker game.

Scramble Mission to Pakxe

About a half hour later, the squadron's Operations Officer burst into the hooch, took a deep breath, and yelled, "Listen up! Clearly, he was excited which was atypical for a guy usually noted for his "cool" under fire. He waited a few seconds for the noise to subside before speaking.

"I need four crews to fly a scramble mission to Pakxe."

Pakxe, Laos was an Air America base just east of Ubon on the Mekong River where the CIA operated its own clandestine war. Standing next to Bob the Ops Officer said, "Bob, are you and Pete able to fly", pointing to the half empty drinks in our hands. Holding up his glass Bob said, "Sure, this is our first".

"Good", he replied, "then saddle up; there's a truck out front."

Several other crews reluctantly agreed and we all ran back to our rooms to change back into our flight suits.

It was around 4:30 PM and my roommate and good friend John had not returned from his afternoon mission. The room was empty and dark since we typically kept our only window covered so we could sleep in the day after returning from night missions. Only the monotonous growl of our aging window AC filled the void. Turning on the overhead light, I quickly slipped out of my civvies and grabbed my sweat-soaked flight suit. Giving it a quick sniff, I realized no one gave a damn how I smelled at this point.

The one-piece Nomex flight suit was informal and comfortable with lots of pockets, but most important, it was fire resistant. Kicking off my shower shoes I slipped into my socks and flight boots and zippered them up in the front. I bolted out of the room and headed for the waiting truck.

Bob, I and several other crews all seemed to arrive about the same time. Bob jumped in the cab with the driver while the rest of us climbed into the bed of the pickup. Moments later the rest of the group arrived and jumped in the back as well. We were pretty well packed in like sardines in a can but in a few minutes, this would turn out to be beneficial. With a grinding noise and a low curse, the young Airman driver jammed the aging OD (olive drab) colored pickup into gear and peeled out; sending gravel flying out behind like so much shrapnel. "Hell", I thought to myself, "it's one thing to die in combat and quite a different thing to die in a car wreck'; although now the distinction seems moot.

VIETNAM 1972:
A TIME BEST FORGOTTEN | 25

Enroute to the flight line, even though packed tightly together, we were tossed around like a rag doll being shaken by an aggravated dog. As the truck careened around the corners, a constant stream of oaths from the driver assaulted us. Clearly the driver had issues with the vehicle he had drawn from the motor pool that day. Perhaps he was responding to the perceived urgency of the moment, but I believe he was deriving some perverse pleasure at scaring the hell out of the officers in back.

Arriving at the equipment room the driver applied the brakes as vigorously as he had the accelerator. Skidding to a stop, we were all thrust forward against the cab. Although some muttered a few oaths, none were directed at the driver. As we all piled out of the pickup, I think we were just grateful to have survived the experience. I'm sure most of us were confident the driver would never make the pages of "Safe Driver" magazine -- if there were such a publication. I remember thinking "that whatever this mission was, it couldn't be as dangerous the ride we just survived".

As we entered the equipment room, I noted several floor fans running at high speed. However, the heat and smell of sweat-soaked gear still permeated the drab interior. The equipment was housed in a long, crudely built, 2" x 4" building with a corrugated metal roof. Filling the room were long steel racks holding the crew's personal flight gear. I moved quickly to my equipment station, identified by a one-inch-wide strip of white medical tape with my last name printed with a black ink marker pen.

I grabbed my chaps, secured it around my waist, and bent over hooking the two halves of each legging together. With a quick upward motion, I zipped each leg up to my crotch. I then grabbed my survival vest, slipping each arm through the armholes and zipped it up the front. The vest was heavy and bulky, supplied with a small survival radio, two extra batteries, first aid kit, chrome plated metal signal mirror, a flare pen with extra 38 caliber-sized flares, a strobe light and several strips of 38 bullets sewed into the canvas webbing. Grabbing my helmet bag from the rack I headed for the exit. A skinny older sergeant, standing near the exit, shoved a loaded Smith & Wesson 38 revolver in my hand saying,

"Sir, don't forget this."

"Thanks," I replied, pushing it into the holster on my left hip.

Climbing into the back of a blue flight line truck, I looked in my helmet bag to verify that my checklist was inside my helmet along with the attached oxygen mask. I'm not sure why I did that. I always stored my checklist in my helmet bag. I removed the blue plastic-covered checklist with its many yellow pages, and slipped it into the right calf pocket of my chaps. The chaps were made of OD green canvas material with internal air bladders. When hooked to the aircraft's pressurization system and pulling heavy Gs (units of gravity), the bladders would inflate squeezing the calves and thighs to prevent blood pooling in the lower legs. This would ensure that some blood remained in the brain to temporarily delay black out or unconsciousness.

On one mission I had either failed to hook my chaps to the aircraft system, or the bayonet connector on my chaps had come uncoupled during the flight. When we pulled out of a steep dive-bombing run, the blood drained from my brain and pooled in my legs. Within seconds my visual world collapsed from normal peripheral vision to a gray tunnel. Although I didn't completely black out, I was certainly on the verge of doing so. In our business, chaps were a lifesaver.

A Briefing Officer from Operations jumped in the truck and handed each of us a few sheets of paper on which were printed the target coordinates, call signs and radio frequencies, etc. On this mission our call sign would be Maple flight. As the truck speed off toward our aircraft, he explained that a company-sized unit of VC had infiltrated onto a Karst (flat topped mountain) overlooking the CIA base at Pakxe and was shelling the base with mortar and rocket rounds. Being only minutes away, Ubon was tasked to destroy this force since there were no other armed and airborne aircraft available. I felt like I was in the 7th Calvary coming to the rescue of a wagon train under attack by hostile Indians. However, this wasn't fun and games or a B rated western; it was a deadly serious situation and friendly forces were dying.

Clearly this wasn't the way we usually started a mission. Under normal circumstances we were given time to study the mission profile, gear up and properly preflight the weapons and aircraft. But this wasn't a normal situation. The 8th Tactical Fighter Wing to which we were attached, did not have a reason to maintain a strip alert flight so this was clearly a "grab and go" scramble mission. We arrived at our aircraft, one of our own F-4Es, which was loaded with 12 finned napalm bombs.

The 8th TFW was the resident wing whose crews were assigned as a 12-month PCS (permanent change of station). Bob and I were a 6-month TDY (Temporary Duty) crew from the 4 TFW stationed at Seymour Johnson AFB, NC. The 8th had the older D models, which lacked the nose-mounted 20mm Vulcan (a large, internal motor driven, multi-barreled Gatling gun mounted below the cockpit). The Crew Chief said the aircraft was prepped for tomorrow's mission but that it had enough fuel to get to and from the target without air refueling. There was no time for the usual preflight.

We scrambled up the ladder, climbed into the cockpit and buckled ourselves into our ejection seats. The chief pulled the ejection seat safety pins and removed the ladder and tossing it to the side of the revetment. The revetments were made of heavy gauge corrugated steel, approximately 10' high, with rear and side walls around 6' wide, filled with dirt and rock. From above they looked like a series of HHHHHH stacked side by side. Backed into each open end of the H-shaped revetment was a fighter. The idea behind these revetments was to prevent an entire line of aircraft blowing up if one was either hit by a sapper's mortar round, or some fuel or ordnance ignition.

Bob started the engines while I turned on the radar and started to program the Inertial Navigation System (INS). Moments later we were cleared to taxi to the ordnance check area at the end of the runway. Bob signaled the crew chief who then pulled the wheel chocks and gave us thumbs up for good luck. As we cleared the revetment the chief cleared us for a 90 degree right turn with an arm signal followed immediately with a hand salute. We both returned his salute and I busied myself trying to get the radar up and running while aligning the INS. Arriving at the holding area, as a Major and the most senior pilot, Bob was flight lead. The munitions team was moving around under the aircraft and wings pulling the safety pins from the bombs and three ejector racks. Moments later the other three aircraft arrived and lined up to our left. The munitions team moved cautiously to each of the other aircraft removing the safety pins from their ordnance.

In the cockpit it was sweltering hot from the afternoon sun. I could only image what it was like for the guys down on the hot pavement with all the additional heat being generated from our engines. The air was foul with the smell of burnt JP-4 fuel from the exhaust. Their sweat soaked fatigues was a clear indication they weren't comfortable campers and couldn't wait for us to depart so they could return to the shade. With an already wet handkerchief, I tried to mop the sweat from my forehead and eyes with only marginal success. I shared the ground crew's desire for us to take off.

With his left arm extended over the canopy rail toward the aircraft to our immediate left, Bob pointed at the pilot. The other pilot gave a thumbs-up in acknowledgement that he was ready to launch. About that time the radio crackled and tower said, "Maple flight, you are cleared for takeoff. Altimeter setting is 29.90, contact departure control on 235.5 MH." "Roger", Bob acknowledged reading back the clearance and releasing the breaks.

Throttling up slowly we taxed onto the right side of the runway while closing our canopies. It would take about five minutes before the cockpit would cool down to our liking. Our wingman lined up on the left side of the runway. Both aircraft were poised side-by-side with about 20 feet between wing tips with both crews looking at one other. Glancing down the runway, the trees at the far end appeared to be wiggling like hula dancers in the heat rising off the concrete. Bob then turned his head to look forward and dipped his head, signaling to the wingman to throttle up to military power. Acceleration was initially gradual but a few seconds later, while racing down the runway side by side, Bob nodded his head again and the engines of both aircraft were throttled into afterburner. A sheet of blue-yellow flame shot 8 or 10 feet out behind # 2's engines and we were thrust back in our seats. With the deafening noise came a rapid increase in the speed. The runway markers were soon an indistinguishable blur as we rocketed by.

With each passing second the end of the runway was growing larger and larger in the cockpit windscreen. I could tell the aircraft was anxious to fly. The heavy bouncing that I felt initially had given way to a smoother ride as the aircraft's weight was lifting off the landing gear. Struts extended and reaching takeoff airspeed, Bob pulled back gently on the stick and we lifted effortlessly into the air. A second or so later a thump and corresponding sharp vibration under our feet signaled the doors closing on an up and locked nose wheel landing gear. Throttling back to military power, the noise and additional thrust produced by the after-burners ceased as we climbed out on the runway heading. With the flaps retracted we started a wide climbing starboard turn to the runway's reciprocal heading.

Approaching the departure end of the runway I could see the other element of two aircraft taking flight. Once airborne they immediately started a steep climbing turn toward us. Minutes later, with their white underbellies showing in their tight rejoining turn, the other element slipped into echelon formation off our right wing. We leveled off at 10,000 feet since a higher altitude would be a waste of valuable fuel. We would be over the target in a few minutes and making a fairly shallow attack so more altitude would be counter-productive.

With the coordinates of Pakxe in the INS, Bob steadied up on the new heading. Refreshing cool air was now filling the cockpit and I pulled off my sweat filled oxygen mask. My afternoon stubble pressing against the sweaty rubber mask was uncomfortable, and at this altitude, oxygen was unnecessary. Then, as we did each mission after takeoff, each aircraft took turns slipping under his wingman checking to be sure all ordinance was secure and there were no hydraulic leaks. Although I never said anything, initially I wondered "what if". What if a bomb or missile was hanging by one shackle? Flying only 20 feet or so under the other plane was a dangerous place to be should anything thing fall off. However, after a few missions I grew complacent and took the maneuver as SOP (standard operating procedure).

However, I never did get accustomed to Bob's habit of rolling inverted on the return flight to collect any nuts and bolts that might fall onto the canopy. During maintenance an occasional nut, bolt, screw etc. would drop on the floor of the cockpit. If they rolled under the seat or fell down into the rudder peddle well, they could go unnoticed and uncollected. Since Bob's job when not flying was as Wing Safety Officer, he knew such loose objects could get jammed in the rudder assembly. However, hanging inverted in my seat wasn't all that comfortable and if not warned in advance, I would have to catch my floating checklist. There was a place on the top of my ejection seat where if the checklist hit it with sufficient force, it would fire my canopy from the aircraft thus initiating my unanticipated ejection. Although we had one of the best ejection seats made, if caught unprepared you could have an arm sheared off by the canopy rail on the side of the cockpit. In such a situation you would bleed to death before hitting the ground. After the first such maneuver, thereafter Bob gave me a "heads up" before initiating it. One time he did that maneuver rolling over our wingman. I still vividly remember the surprised look, or perhaps shocked look is a more apt term, on the wingman's face as he looked up and saw us hanging inverted, canopy to canopy, only 80 feet or so above him. The following photo illustrates this.

Whether a Lieutenant or Lt Colonel, pilots sometimes need to vent their pent-up emotions after a difficult mission. While flying up north on an earlier mission with a young pilot, we had taken on too much fuel during our post-strike air refueling and would be landing heavy. As a result, we were cleared to conduct mock air-to-air combat maneuvers enroute to base to burn down the weight. At one point we climbed through 46,000 feet at mach 1.1. "Not too shabby for a 1957 designed bird," I thought.

Figure: Six degree climb thru 46,000 feet at mach 1.1

Still heavy he dove down and leveled off at tree top level then started skimming 15 feet or so above the Mekong River at Mach 1 (speed of sound). You could see the shock wave on the surface of the river turning the dark brown surface a milky brown, like cream mixing in a cup of black coffee. On a straight stretch of the river just south of Savannakhet, we overturned some terrified fisherman paddling across the river. He never saw or heard us coming. I can only imagine the noise and shock wave he felt after we passed only a few feet over his head. However, at that altitude and speed a bird strike could have ruined our entire day.

After landing, and without explaining why, I told the ops officer to never team me up with that pilot again. I had two young children and a wife at home and being shot at daily was enough drama in my life without going out looking for more. I guess I was, and still am, just a 'woose' (not inclined to take unnecessary risks). But I have strayed from the current mission, again!!!

Once we checked each other over for hung ordnance, we all assumed a loose finger four combat formation. [Finger four refers to the position of the aircraft if you were to fold your thumb under the palm of one hand and look down at the tips of your other fingers. We borrowed this formation from the German Luftwaffe]. Over the radio Departure Control said, "Maple Flight, you have closing traffic, 20 miles 10 o'clock low." A quick glance at the radarscope confirmed the information. A minute later we passed over and slightly to the right of a flight of four brown and green camouflaged F-4s returning to base. I silently wondered if my roommate and friend John was in one of those birds. The thought was quickly suppressed, however, as we busied ourselves making sure we had accomplished everything on the checklist.

It seemed like only a few minutes later that the FAC [forward air controller] came up on frequency. "Maple flight, this is Eagle Eye, how do you read?"

"Five-by" replied Bob, "ETA on station with flight of four in five minutes."

"Roger that" replied Eagle Eye, "what's your ordinance?"

Bob responded, "We each have 12 finned Nape and two of us have 20mm guns."

"Great", the FAC replied, "let me brief you on the situation here. You can't miss the target. It is a big ass flat-topped karst covered with trees on all sides, about 2 clicks (kilometers) northeast of the base. When you get here set your perch (orbit altitude) at 6,000 feet so you all can get a good look at the target. Charlie has some mortars on the top and I've seen lots of troops all around the base as well. All they seem to have is small arms so if you swing wide you should stay out of trouble. Number one, if you would, make your run in southwest to northeast and aim for the middle of the mountain. Then moving around the hill counterclockwise, have number 2 run in 90 degrees to that on a heading of around 310. If you each catch a different quarter of the hill it ought to get the job done. When that's over have the two guys with the guns rake the top and anything else that's left. Do you copy?"

"Roger Eagle Eye' replied Bob. "Maple Flight, when we cross over the base, we will set up a left-hand wheel at 6,000. I will make the first run in from the southwest, # 2 you follow from the southeast, # 3 you follow from the northeast, etc. Everyone understand?"

"Roger 2",

"Roger 3",

"Roger 4", were the replies.

"Eagle Eye, I have the base in sight. Where are you?" radioed Bob.

"Maple, I have you in sight." I am about one click southeast at tree top level. Don't worry; I plan to stay well out of the way. You are cleared in hot at your discretion."

"Roger Eagle Eye. Maple flight, get you're spacing. This will be a 'one-pass haul ass' run. Arm them up. Maple 3, since you have a gun, I will sweep the east side of the mountain and when I'm clear you take the west side. I want to avoid sending any rounds in the direction of the base."

"Maple 3, Roger" he replied.

We then started a gradual descent to 6,000' and, not knowing how high the mortar round could go, swung wide of the base to avoid being hit. From our orbit I couldn't see the enemy. Our offset was too far and our speed too great. Anyway, I suspect they had "hunkered down" in holes or caves when we started orbiting their position. I know I would if I was in their sandals. For all I knew they might even have been shooting at us. However, without the telltale streak of tracer rounds I was blissfully ignorant of their presence or activity.

Bob went 'Armed' and 'Bombs Ripple' on the weapon select switch. As the compass needle approached 270 degrees, Bob called over the radio "Maple One rolling in" and we started a gradual diving port turn. When stable on a heading of 045 degrees Bob put the piper mid-way up the side of the mountain and adjusted to a 30-degree dive angle. The mountain rapidly grew in view as we approached and Bob squeezed the trigger while simultaneously pulling out of the shallow dive. This created a wider disbursal pattern on impact.

As we screamed over the top of the karst I caught a momentary glimpse of the mortars and their crew as they ducked for cover. I also caught a glimpse of at least half dozen men with AK-47 assault rifles firing at us. We rapidly reached orbit altitude and Bob maneuvered the aircraft in such a way as to resume the normal spacing between the other members of the flight. Over my left shoulder I saw a blazing inferno with rolling black smoke swirling skyward. Number 2 then called in from the southeast. I watched with a curious mixture of horror and fascination. There was more fire and smoke as Maple 2 pulled off. Shortly thereafter Maples 3 & 4 made their respective runs leaving the sides of the mountain a blazing inferno.

Napalm is such a horrible, yet effective, weapon. Many nations had signed an international accord to ban its use, but the US had not. I became aware of movement on the upper edges of the target. "Hell," I exclaimed, "it looks like someone kicked a fireant mound." Enemy soldiers, some on fire and many others trying to escape the searing heat and flames, were seeking refuge on the top. "Maple One, this is Eagle Eye. Do you see what I see?" the FAC said with equal amazement.

"Roger Eagle Eye, position yourself either north or south of the target so you don't get hit. I'm rolling in from the east."

"Roger Maple One' replied the FAC, "I'm clear."

As the compass needle approached 100 degrees Bob made a diving port turn rolling out on a heading of roughly 270 degrees.

"Switching to Guns," he said matter of factly.

Steadying up the gun sight on the flat-topped mountain, he squeezed the trigger. Both a tremendous roar and a vibration shook the plane as a fusillade of 20mm bullets streamed out in front of the plane. The top of the mountain erupted in a massive cloud of red dust and vegetation. I could only imagine what a 3" long bullet the diameter of a quarter would do to a man. A second later we skimmed over the top of the hill. Fire, black smoke and red dust obscured the devastation I am sure had occurred below. Although we still had enough rounds to make a second run our fuel was getting low. Anyway, a second run would have been overkill in my estimation. Maple 3 made his strafing run and pulled off the target.

Bob came up on the radio and said "Eagle Eye, Maple flight is RTB. Good working with you."

"Roger Maple Flight – great job and thanks!"

The flight rejoined, checked each other for any possible hung ordnance or battle damage, and headed home. Reflecting on the carnage we had inflicted, stirred both feelings of accomplishment and revolution. But then, that's war!

"**Pete, turn down the TV**!" Karen yelled. "Charlie and Linda across the street can probably hear it!" Karen had been after me for months to get a hearing aid but I have been dragging my feet. I guess it would be just another thing to remind me I'm getting old. Karen's voice had, however, mercifully broken the spell of that day 37 years ago. As far as days go, **that had been a good day** for me. We had landed safely with no holes in either the plane or ourselves. In light of that, it was a Great Day. Someone once said "any landing you can walk away from is a good landing." By that definition it was a good landing. We accomplished the mission; that was that!

And the war would go on. For me, however, memory of the day's events has haunted me at night for years.

My thoughts reflected on that "good day" assessment. If that was a good day, what the heck was a Bad Day? Then bits and pieces of day 12,320 began to coalesce. Although I had struggled over the years to keep the memories from surfacing, it was a losing battle. Far too many sleepless nights over the years were spent wrestling with these memories. Now how did the following mission in October 1972 start?

Dawn of a Bad Day for Friend and Foe Alike

It started with the annoying clatter of John's alarm clock bringing me out of a rather fitful slumber. Our dark, dreary room, rudely replaced thoughts of my wife and children back in North Carolina. Thankfully the quarters of the flight crews were all air-conditioned so we could get adequate rest. John silenced the clock and the room was again still with the exception of the monotonous, grating noise of the aging window air conditioner. I thought "By its sound, it may not see us through our remaining months on station. Oh well, [pause], I'll deal with that if or when it happens". A few minutes later I heard John's feet hit the floor and his fumbling attempts to find the switch on the night-light. Once on, it provided just enough light with which to dress yet not so much that it would be too disturbing to me. He grabbed his towel and shaving kit and left the room for the latrine. Alone, I tried to regain my thoughts of home and family.

I must have fallen back to sleep for a while because my next conscious thought occurred with the morning sun struggling to pass through the draped window and the noise from guys going past my door for the latrine.

Although slightly out of focus I could make out by the clock on the bed stand that it was 0810 hours. John was long gone as I headed to the latrine at the end of our building. The thundering roar of afterburners from the flight line announced the launch of his morning mission. The first two aircraft had just gone "wheels in the well" as they appeared over the buildings ahead and the noise translated into rattling windows and vibration in the sidewalk. I wondered if John was in that element but the though quickly vanished as the need to empty my bladder took precedence.

The latrine, more often referred to as "the John or the Head" for some obscure reason, was full of steam, men with white towels wrapped around their mid sections shaving, and the noise of Leroy singing in the shower. "What did he have to sing about?" I wondered. Leroy was no Pavarotti but you had to give him credit for trying. He was a large, hairy-chested, bachelor in his late 20's or early 30's. I think he chased nearly every "Stew" (stewardess) who occasionally arrived at the Officer's Club on one of the contract Air America birds bring in, or taking out, troops. On one occasion he showed up in the squadron hooch around 11 PM with a rather attractive Stewardess. Hell, if she was a "round eye" and breathing she would be attractive to nearly all the guys with whom I was acquainted. One can only speculate that his "upbeat" demeanor signified a satisfying evening with his date.

Inside the latrine, all the commodes were neatly lined up against one wall and the sinks on the opposite, like planes on the flight line. The group shower was centered at the far end. I pulled off my towel, sat down on an empty commode and picked up a discarded newspaper from the floor. Privacy was a luxury of the past. We slept, ate, flew, s̲hit, s̲howered, s̲haved, (the triple "s") and at times, wept or got drunk together. It was a marriage of necessity as it were. Once you got use to this "togetherness", however, the arrangement made for easier communication and mutual BS.

Returning to my room I put on my flight suit and headed to the Officers Club for breakfast. Although John and I shared a room, we seldom seemed to fly at the same time or even on the same mission. However, we did share a similar experience having both been Strategic Air Command (SAC) B-52 Navigator-Bombardiers on our previous assignment. I had been stationed with the 99th Bomb Wing at Westover AFB in Springfield, Massachusetts and John had been at Ramey AFB on Puerto Rico. My mission then was to carry 4 Mark 28FIY1 hydrogen bombs east of the Ural Mountains and drop them on missile silos that would probably be empty by the time I arrived. Although empty, Russian silos were designed to be reloaded for a second launch thus justifying their destruction.

Reflecting back on my "nuc-carrying" days in SAC, I remembered a sobering moment for my first wife. Each Strategic Air Command bomber base equipped with EWO (Emergency War Order) tasked aircraft, had a similar facility at the end of the runway adjacent to a special parking area for B-52s. This parking area (called the Christmas tree because of its appearance from above), was enclosed by high chain link fencing with a controlled access gate. Armed guards walking with dogs patrolled the six cocked (nuclear loaded) aircraft 24-hours a day year-round in all kinds of weather. On this particular occasion my family met me in the parking area just outside the alert facility fence and only about fifty yards from one of the bombers. While sitting in the car, a munitions crew arrived to change out the quad pack of H-bombs (we carried 4 to an aircraft). When they pulled the canvas cover off the cart my wife saw these four 18"' diameter by 12' long silver bombs. Since I never discussed our mission or the weapons we carried, I was somewhat surprised she knew what they were. I guess it was the "wives network" which provided her the background intel. She suddenly gasped at the realization that she was only a few yards away from 28 hydrogen bombs; 4 in each of the 6 parked bombers and the four replacements they were about to exchange for routine maintenance. I believe it was only then that she fully comprehended the serious nature of our mission and its impact on our family. After all, we were then living on base about a mile away.

If we received the "Go Code" (attack the enemy), we would be essentially on a one-way mission. On my first tour of alert as a navigator it was my job to assist Larry, the bombardier, in his pre-flight of the "nucs". I noticed that the bomb rack only filled the front part of the bomb bay while the rest of the bay was empty. After some reflection I said, "Larry, since we have to fly all that way to the Soviet Union, why not carry another rack of four bombs?" Larry looked at me and grinned saying,

"Pete, they aren't that confident we will reach the first four targets and don't want to waste any additional weapons." That realization really struck home. Although we had all these "post-strike" egress routes, bases, and plans, the probability of our managing to escape Soviet airspace was statistically nil. The strategic planners knew it and now so did I. No sense worrying my family, they would probably die from a Soviet missile warhead before I ever left US airspace.

My thoughts returned to 1972 and the conventional war we were now fighting. I was on the schedule for the afternoon mission with a 1 PM show. Since I had been part of a select group tasked to plan Linebacker missions, I already knew where we were headed. The mission was to be a 60-plane attack on targets along the northeast railroad that ran between the Chinese border and Hanoi. Aircraft from several different bases in Thailand were to join up off the east coast of Vietnam. It was to be a mixture of attack aircraft, MiG cap birds from the 555 TFW (Triple nickel) at Udorn, some F105 Wild Weasel missile suppression aircraft, and KC-135 tankers. The profile called for a flight across Vietnam to "feet wet" over the South China Sea, then we would turn north along the coast to our refueling track. Once in the Haiphong area we would head NW along "Thud Ridge" until we split up the formation to hit various targets along the NE rail road.

The Rules of Engagement really prevented planning a mission that would give us the element of surprise. Our ingress and egress routes were dictated, in great measure, by enemy defenses and politics. A cardinal rule, however, was "don't over fly the Chinese border." We didn't want to provide China with an excuse to overtly enter the conflict. Although they were already providing logistical and engineering support, and probably technical assistance in the form of limited manpower, at least we weren't confronted with their huge land force. I wouldn't have been surprised if some of the MiG pilots were

Chinese since Russian pilots manned many of the fighters during the Korean War. As we approached targets in the Hanoi area, the North Vietnamese fighters would typically scramble and head for the safety of Chinese airspace. On several missions, crews reported seeing them orbiting just a few miles north of the border as if daring us to enter Chinese airspace.

Our predictability was costing us aircraft, mission after mission. Climbing off a target, usually a railroad or highway bridge near the Chinese border, our attacking aircraft would turn south. This maneuver would expose the engine heat source to attacking MiGs coming out of China. All too frequently the enemy would slip into our 6 o'clock position (behind us) while climbing out of the target area and struggling for altitude and airspeed. With an overtake speed advantage, the MiGs were exposed for only a few brief seconds while they locked on, fired their Atoll heat seeking missiles, and streaked at near supersonic speed past the formation for the AAA (anti-aircraft artillery) protection of down town Hanoi. However, today we had planned a surprise tactic which might give us a slight advantage.

After breakfast I stopped by the mailroom in hopes there would be a letter. "None today" was the clerk's response. Disappointed, I returned to my room to write one home. I knew things were probably OK but a letter, no matter how mundane, was always a welcomed event. They served as a thread of continuity and sanity in this period of turmoil and insanity. Business as usual back home had a stabilizing effect on my hectic, and at times frantic, life. My daughter Terri was 9 and my son Eric a toddler of 1. I would print a few sentences in each letter so Terri could read it herself and then directed the rest to my wife. "How is everyone? Are you paying all the bills? Is everything OK with the house, etc.", were some topics frequently discussed. I seldom, if ever, discussed the missions or the ever-present danger we faced each day. It would serve no productive purpose other than scare them when there was nothing they could do about the circumstances. Besides, Walter Cronkite and the other newscasters bombarded them with commentary and photos every night. I finished the letter and sealed it in an envelope. It wasn't very long, but at least they would get something. It was getting close to the time to report for the afternoon mission briefing, so I dropped the letter off at the mailroom enroute to Operations.

There was nothing unusual about the briefing or the mission package. It was essentially the mission several of us had planned the day before. Each aircraft in our flight of four would be dropping 18 Mark 82 (streamlined 500 lb GP [general purpose] bombs) on a railroad bridge five clicks (kilometers) or so south of China. We would then make a hard climbing port turn off the target to prevent over-flying the Chinese border. Our Intel indicated that there was a very strong likelihood MiG's would attempt to shoot us down while we were climbing off the target. In anticipation of this, the other flight of four aircraft would hit a target about 30 miles to the southwest and turn north east toward us on their climb out. In this way they would be head-to-head with any aircraft coming out of China after our flight. I certainly hoped this scissor tactic would work. Bob and I put the mission materials back in the folder and headed to the equipment building for our gear and transportation to the flight line.

Pre-Flight

Arriving at our aircraft and seeing all the bombs attached to the three pylons, six on the center and six on each wing ejector rack, made you wonder how the plane would ever get airborne. Our 2-man fighter carried more bombs than the 10-man B17 bomber of WWII, but far less than the 108 bombs carried by the 6-man B-52. The Crew Chief handed Bob the 781-maintenance binder, which he reviewed.

"We've got a CND (Could Not Duplicate) on an intermittent Com Radio", he said.

"Just what we need", he muttered sarcastically.

"I hope it doesn't act up today."

CND meant that a previous crew had some problems with the radio but maintenance could not duplicate nor fix the malfunction. Since replacing the radio required removing the canopy and pulling the ejection seat to get to it, they would have to follow up later when time permitted. It was only a few years later that they started designing aircraft with components that could be accessed through the side of the fuselage like a chest of drawers.

While Bob checked the IFF (Identification Friend or Foe) setting, landing gear and control surfaces, I check the arming wires and fuses on each bomb, pulling the shackle safety pins as I went. I then looked over the directional fins of the two-radar directed AIM-7s Sparrows (Air Intercept Missile) mounted on the belly of the aircraft. Everything appeared normal so we each took a quick 'wiz' at the back of the revetment before climbing aboard. The mission was scheduled to last about three hours and that's about as long as my bladder would last. I always tried to avoid drinking anything for a few hours before a mission to reduce the problem.

Before climbing into the cockpit, I made a quick check of the ejection seat, circuit breakers, and other electronic equipment. I then climbed in and strapped up. With engine start time approaching, the chief started the air cart and climbed up on the engine intake to remove our ejection seat safety pins. There had been times when a seat, without an installed safety pin, accidentally fired while on the ground killing the maintenance or crewman involved. After the canopy is jettisoned, the seat is propelled up a set of rails via a sequenced series of rockets. The sequencing was designed to reduce spinal compression fractures during ejection. On one occasion a maintenance technician, sitting on one of the ejection seats, was killed when he was accidentally ejected into the roof of the hanger. The British-made Martin Baker ejection seat in the F-4 was a very reliable system, but it couldn't anticipate human screw-ups. However, despite some hazards, ejection seats were normally a lifesaver. During WWII, very few B-17 crews were able to get out of their aircraft once all the forces started to act on the tumbling or spinning aircraft. Our system would blow off the canopy, rocket the occupant out of the aircraft, release his lap belt, toss him out of the seat, provide him with emergency oxygen from the bottle in the parachute pack, and deploy the parachute automatically at a preset altitude in the event he was unconscious. A very comforting thought if you found yourself in trouble and your aircraft was coming apart.

On today's mission our squadron commander was also the mission commander of our flight of four F-4Ds. We were number three in the first flight, with Bob being element led. Should the commander flying # 1 become disabled or shot down, Bob would be tasked to take control of the flight and mission. Another flight of four would follow us closely, but once in the general target area they would split off and hit their target some 30 miles or so farter to the southwest.

At start engine time, the ground cart started the engines spinning. Bob cracked the throttles sending fuel to the engines while simultaneously igniting the mixture. A few minutes later both engines were running smoothly and the instruments reflected normal operation. All the aircraft taxied out of their respective revetments like a well-choreographed dance routine. The rest of the taxi and take off occurred as planned and each flight of four headed east toward Vietnam. We were light on fuel in order to permit taking off with a maximum bomb load, so a pre-strike air refueling (AR) was critical. Today's AR track was over the South China Sea paralleling the Vietnamese coastline. So far everything was normal and uneventful. Since we were # 3, the flight lead in # 1 took care of all the radio calls and coordination. All we had to do was sit back and fly.

Loran Missions

My mind drifted back to the very long and busy Loran runs over South Vietnam employed when bad weather prevented dive-bombing attacks. Perhaps because of my previous training as a B-52 navigator-bombardier, I was selected to lead many of these missions. Loran was a system that triangulated your position by evaluating the electronic signals from three widely spaced transmitters on the ground. A special ballistics and navigational computer on board would interpret these signals and fix your position. I don't think it was anywhere near as accurate as today's GPS systems, but it was better than nothing. A typical Loran mission profile would start with a four-ship launch, all with the same type aircraft and bomb load, and strike a specific target. I would verbally drop the original flight by programming the coordinates of the target, and Bob would center the PDI (Pilot's Data Indicator). Over the radio, I would count down the TG (time to go) backward from 10 to 0 at which time I would call "Pickle, Pickle, Pickle". All aircraft would be flying in loose finger-four formation and release in straight and level flight.

Figure: Loran drop during Monsoon season

The bombs would disappear through the lower cloud deck and we would never see the results. After the originating aircraft dropped, Bob and I would head for a tanker while the other three would RTB (Return to Base). Once refueled, we would receive instructions from the ground to hit a new set of target coordinates. Our control would tell us where to rendezvous with new group of attacking aircraft. Most rendezvous points were TACAN range and bearings off Channel 66 located at Da Nang AB. On a busy day we could be airborne for six or more hours.

On one occasion four Navy birds, 2 A-7s with 750 lb bombs and 2 F-4s with slick 500 lb bombs, joined up with us. The ballistic parameters were different for both types of ordnance but ground told me to make only one run. I split the difference between the two ballistic inputs and programmed the on-board computer. I called the aircraft on each wing telling them we were IP inbound as Bob lined us up on the proper heading. The four aircraft tucked in close on each wing and we all "eyeballed" one another. Enroute to the target I read off the checklist item "Arm your ordnance". Each aircraft diligently replied "Roger" and I started the count down at 10 seconds TG. At my command "Pickle, pickle, pickle" the bombs came off three of the four aircraft. I noticed # 4 still had his ordnance so I said "# 4 you still have your bombs" to which I heard his reply "shit" followed by the immediate release of all his bombs. To this day I am confident he had not armed his system as instructed, but then armed and released them some 6 seconds or so down track. Six seconds delay, at over 400 feet per second, put those bombs way down tract. I wondered "Who, or what, was under those bombs he released so late?" However, no one ever said anything, so I guess we were hitting a jungle target and no friendly forces were hurt. I've always wondered about that, however. Unfortunately, collateral damage and fratricide are occasional unintended occurrences in warfare.

Air Refueling

My mind snapped back to the current mission. On reaching our turning point over the South China Sea just east of Hue, lead turned port to a heading of 360 (due North). I ran the radar range out and painted the tankers around 55 miles coming toward us on our reciprocal heading. Bob ran a quick pre-contact check and announced he had a visual on them at 11 o'clock as the takers started a port turn to our heading. The lead tanker rolled out about a quarter mile ahead of us. Lead was the first to hook up. In a few minutes he had topped off his tanks and moved down and to the side so his wingman could refuel. Then it was our turn. We slipped effortlessly into a trail position about 20 feet below, and slightly behind, the tanker. The director lights farther up on the tanker's fusalage were difficult to see but Bob, and most fighter pilots, flew visual formation during day missions. We were cleared into "contact position" by the boomer. As we moved forward, the boomer extended the telescoping boom revealing red, yellow and green markings on the silver pipe extending over our cockpit. The boom had two short wing-like surfaces on the end, which would pivot in response to the Boomer's joystick. With the joystick he delicately maneuvered the tip of the nozzle only inches over our

canopy. A thump announced that the boom had seated itself in the receptacle behind me and the swishing sound of transferring fuel could be heard. Looking up I could see the boomer on his stomach lying on his couch only a few meters away. He was intent on the transfer. In the meantime, Bob kept the aircraft in position using the green marking on the boom as a reference. When the fuel transfer was complete, the boomer disconnected, retracted and flew the boom up and out of the way. We slipped down and off to one side as # 4 moved into position. Bob closed the refueling doors located on the top of the aircraft just behind the cockpit. So far everything was uneventful. Perhaps it would turn out to be a good day. Reaching the end of the air-refueling tract the tankers turned south toward safety, and we proceeded north toward Haiphong and an unknown afternoon.

Figure: Boomer's view passing gas

As we approached land, I turned on our RAW (Radar Attack and Warning) gear. It served as a poor man's frequency jamming device and would provide us a directional warning strobe on a small screen in the rear cockpit. To be sure we were aware of a threatening problem, it would also produce a distinctive squeal in our headsets. Haiphong harbor appeared off our left wing and I could see several freighters off-loading supplies. Back in April President Nixon was determined to mine the harbor in spite of a CIA study which indicated supplies would only be redirected to overland or airlift routes making mining risky and counterproductive. Ever present was concern that attacking the ships would kill Soviet crews and risk further escalation. US troop withdrawals had resulted in only around 6,000 Americans still in country. Constant political interference and civil disapproval at home played into the enemy's hands. To offset the military disadvantage facing the ARVN forces, large deployment of tactical air from the US and other overseas locations to bases throughout Thailand was made from April – October. The strategy called for massive sorties against targets in the north. So here Bob and I are on today's mission, part of that initiative.

Along Thud Ridge to the Target

Approaching our turning point in an extended finger four tactical formation, lead dipped his wing signaly our element to change positions in preparation for the turn. Bob and our wingman dipped down and slid under the leader and his wingman. Then both wingmen slid into their respective positions. The flight then turned to a heading of around 310 and headed inland along Thud Ridge. [Thud Ridge was so named because of the number of F-105s (called Thuds by many) that had been shot down along the ridge.]

The sky started filling with black puffs of smoke from the 100 mm AAA batteries along the coast and lining Thud Ridge. With each puff there was a mass of high-speed shrapnel that could tear into a plane's engine and fuel tanks. We climbed higher to see if we could get over the flak. It took the enemy a few valuable minutes to realize the altitude change and reset the fuses. Once shells starting exploding at our altitude again, lead took us back down to around 15,000 feet. Looking up, I could see the black puffs above us as well as feel the concussion of their detonation. We were about half way to the target when the flak subsided. "Was that a good sign or bad," I wondered. I searched the sky to the north both visually and with our on-board radar, for possible MiGs coming out of China. However, I didn't see anything. The MiG 21 was small and hard to see even under ideal circumstances.

A high pitch squeal in my headset made me instantly realize the flak had stopped for the SAMs (Surface to Air Missiles), not the MiGs. They didn't want to shoot down their own airborne missiles. Suddenly the RAW gear showed a strobe around 10 o'clock. "Bob, I've got a strobe at 10 o'clock low?" Bob strained to see the missile for a minute then he picked up a smoke trail headed our way. Once you saw the missile our defensive tactic was to position the aircraft so the missile was at our 10 or 2 o'clock position. Then it became a game of chicken. The objective was to dive at precisely the right moment when the missile was too close to effectively correct its flight path. We had large horizontal stabilizers with which to affect a negative G pushover maneuver, while the missile only had small control surfaces. Push over too soon and the missile can adjust and hit you; push too late and you are hamburger. Timing was critical and the "pucker factor" was high.

It was hard to say which of the four aircraft in our flight was its specific target, but the missile was getting larger by the second. "Now" the flight leader called excitedly into the radio and all four pilots pushed the stick to the instrument panel with everyone's vision riveted on the incoming missile. Although traveling at well over a 1,000 mph, my mind appears to have switched into slow motion. As the missile loomed ever larger, it then appeared to drift slowly over our starboard wing. The mind could play funny tricks. It was close -- too close -- and it was painted white, not camouflaged green. I guess a load of them had just come off the Russian freighters and they didn't have time to paint them. I stared at the passing SA-2 missile in awe. It looked like a white telephone pole and I could see black writing in places on the missile. Then, as it passed to our 5 o'clock position, there was a violent explosion. The proximity fuse had detonated the missile a millisecond too late. In that second it had traveled several hundred feet past us and the shrapnel had harmlessly gone behind our descending flight. We were now down to 12,000 feet. Lead violently pulled out of the descent and we all scrambled to get back up to our altitude and out of the AAA envelope.

We had just managed to climb about 1500 feet when the RAW gear signaled a second launch. It wasn't from the same launch sight, however. It was off the nose where none of us could see it.

We knew that they frequently fired a volley of three missiles at a target. Following lead, we made a hard turn to the right about 40 degrees and leveled at around 14,000 feet.

"I got another one", someone in the flight yelled. "It's at 11 o'clock".

Lead turned further right and we all searched for the incoming missile.

"I don't have it," said Lead in a rasping voice. "Whoever has it call the maneuver?"

In what seemed like only a second later, someone yelled in the radio, "Take it down!" We all repeated the same maneuver performed a minute earlier and the second missile passed off our left wing but for some reason never detonated. I don't know about the other guys but by now my flight suit was ringing wet with sweat and my eyes stung from its salt. We now recovered at around 10,000 feet and all hell broke loose from the flak guns. Black clouds of searing hot metal were flying in all directions as we scrambled for more altitude. The flak eventually tapered off as we were now about 20 miles farther NW and probably out of their range. Our sister flight of four aircraft had already split off to hit their target farther south. Lead told us to take spacing and slip into trail. We wouldn't be orbiting over the target with each taking turns rolling in. This would be a follow the leader, "one pass haul ass" run.

The target coordinates were in the INS and I crosschecked lead's heading to be sure all was well. The radio chatter had subsided and Bob and I were straining to see any enemy aircraft. If they came at us today, they would be coming from China somewhere between 2 and 3 o'clock off the right side of the nose. Even though visibility was clear, trying to see a small MiG 21 was a daunting task. We descended to 14,000 feet and leveled off. The border was rapidly approaching and Bob started looking at 10 o'clock low for the railroad bridge we were assigned to destroy. I kept scanning to the right of the aircraft but saw nothing but blue sky and puffy clouds.

Lead called out "Target in sight – One's in".

We were about 20 seconds in trail behind # 2 to avoid flying into any shrapnel from his exploding ordnance during our dive. Bob racked the aircraft over in a sharp left hand diving turn rolling out on a heading of 290 degrees. The HSI indicated he had a 40-degree dive angle so he made a few adjustments to get 45-degrees. I shifted from "look out" to the instruments and called out altimeter readings so Bob could concentrate on keeping the piper on the target. Reaching release altitude I called Pickle, Pickle, Pickle on intercom and a split-second latter I felt the aircraft shutter as the entire load of eighteen 500-pound bombs were kicked off the ejector racks.

Bob snatched the stick back in a violent motion and as the aircraft shuttered in response to the change in direction my G-suit inflated and my helmet and mask slide down my sweat-covered face. "So far nothing unusual" I thought. Since I was focusing on the instruments during the dive neither Bob nor I saw any AAA. I'm sure there were several sentries down in the general target area unloading their AK 47s at us but none appeared to have hit us. Bob rolled the aircraft to the left and shoved the throttles into after burner as we struggled to gain both airspeed and altitude. Seconds later we stabilized in a more gradual climbing left hand turn toward our egress heading of 120 degrees. We were going to back track along Thud Ridge with all its SAMs and AAA but that was the closest route to the relative safety of the Gulf of Tonkin. Just as I was about to heave a sigh of relief a voice on guard frequency made us catch our breath.

"Purple flight, you have a bandit at your six!"

That is a heart stopping radio transmission no crew member wants to hear but is grateful for the "heads up". Since we were still in a climbing left turn, I swiveled my body to the right trying to see the threat. "Was he after us or one of the other members in the flight" I wondered. Then, out of the corner of my eye I caught a glimpse of him about two miles behind as he emerged from our 6.

"He's at our 5 o'clock closing fast," I shouted into the intercom.

I don't think Bob saw him at that moment but there was little else he could do than to pull as many Gs as possible in our left turn. Hopefully, this would cause the missile to break any lock it may have had on our heat signature. To roll out of our left turn or turn right would only simplify the MiG's tracking solution and result in our destruction.

The aircraft shuttered under the increased G force. The forces on me made it difficult to keep the MIG in sight. That problem would be solved a second or two later, however.

Now here is where the mind plays tricks and slows down time again. Up to this point everything appeared normal if not in high speed. However, at this point it was as if events shifted into slow motion. Apparently, the MiG pilot had us in his sights and perhaps his heat seeking Atoll missile system had us "locked up". It was difficult to tell since there was no warning indication from our RAW system. At this split second in time, however, I suspect he saw the black smoke trailing from the four F-4s coming off their target farther south as they headed right at him. Most of the North Vietnamese pilots flew under strict guidance from their ground control counterpart and their attack profiles appeared to be relatively inflexible. Confronted with a new and unanticipated tactic by our forces, he had to think for himself and react within seconds. Fortunately for us, he made the decision to go defensive vs. finish his attack. Immediately he performed an energy-conserving high-speed yo-yo (a maneuver designed to trade off his high speed overtake velocity for altitude). He would then be able to trade off that altitude moments later for airspeed by hopefully diving out of harms way.

I looked over the right wing and he appeared to drift into formation with us. For a second or two the enemy pilot traded glances with Bob and me while we were both in a left turn. He then appeared to roll out of his climbing turn and the separation distance between our two aircraft rapidly increased. I was oblivious to everything else for those brief seconds with my attention riveted on this "near miss" we had experienced. Less than three seconds later I felt a mild concussion and the MiG disappeared in an explosive fireball. Large parts of the aircraft with its pilot, each covered with burning fuel, tumbled momentarily in a slightly diverging formation with us. I was awestruck by the unfolding drama as my former attacker died in what I hoped was a quick and painless death. Still in slow motion, I could not help but look down off our left wing to see his country, perhaps his home and his family thousands of feet below.

Just a rapidly as these events had unfolded, seconds later the sky was a pastel blue punctuated with puffy clouds. We rolled out on our egress heading and altitude. All four in our flight were safe, sound and headed "feet wet".

"Bob, are you OK" I asked.

"Ya, but that was a close call" he replied.

I thought that his comment was a colossal understatement. To me it was a life-altering moment seldom experienced by most. Of the hundreds of thousands of men and women who served in Viet Nam, only around 10% or so ever faced death or killed anyone.

I mused at a statement Winston Churchill had once made, "There is nothing more exhilarating in life than to be shot at and missed." My mind flashed back to the dead pilot and his country lying far below. I couldn't help but question why we as Americans were there, what we were attempting to accomplish -- and my role in the entire fiasco. To me it appeared to be an internal civil war and we were hell bent on preserving the status quo of a corrupt government. I guess it was just another example of our containment policy that propelled us into war in Korea two decades earlier.

Headed Feet Wet

As if we hadn't experienced enough drama for one day, an excited call over the radio broke into my silent thoughts. It was a Wild Weasel's [an aircraft engaged in SAM suppression] wingman calling for a possible water rescue for the F-105 crew. Apparently the 'Thud' had taken flak from either a SAM or an AAA shell. A small fire had filled the cockpit with smoke and both blinded crewmembers were getting critical heading, altitude and air speed information from their wingman. Their only engine was damaged, losing power, and threatening to come apart and possibly blow up.

The two aircraft were somewhere ahead of us on a descending course trying to reach the water. If they were to eject now, at best they would become POWS and at worst killed by some irate farmer or local militia. They were banking on the aircraft holding together until they got "feet wet" where our Navy might rescue them. Nearly all radio chatter from within our formation had ceased except for that from the stricken flight. Although we were not experiencing any AAA on our way outbound, black puffs of smoke at our 1 o'clock indicated that the enemy was determined to shoot down both stricken aircraft in that formation before they could reach the coast. Their descending altitude only enhanced the enemy's chances of success.

Finally, we could see the coastline ahead and the F-105 wingman called out they were feet wet with a few thousand feet to spare. Both men in the stricken aircraft punched out and over the radio I heard,

"I have two good chutes".

The wingman apparently circled the men as they splashed down and climbed into their bright yellow life rafts.

"Any flight in the area please provide MiG cap. I'm Bingo (low on fuel) and need to head for a tanker."

About 5 minutes later we reached our turn point over the water and started south toward the post AR tanker. Looking down to his right Bob said, "Hey, I think I see the rafts below!" I set our coordinates into a target window on the INS and asked "Bob, do you see any MIG CAP over them?" "No," he replied. He then called out on our tactical frequency

"Purple 1 this is 3".

"Go three" was the response from our flight/squadron commander.

"I and my wingman can give those guys cover. I have fuel for 10 minutes or so. Request permission to depart the formation" replied Bob.

There was a pause.

"Negative 3, someone farther back in the stream will cover them" led responded.

"Yeh, but who?" Bob replied over intercom.

However, over the radio he replied,

"Roger, 3 out."

Bob and I grumbled a bit about the decision but fell into silence as we headed for the tanker and safety. It would only be hours later that we would all find out the regrettable consequences of that seemingly simple decision.

Figure: Air Refueling

After checking each other over for battle damage, I felt the stick shake.

I responded, "Roger, I've got it."

Having once been a smoker myself, I knew how good that cigarette must have been for Bob after all we had just experienced. To this day I'm not sure how he, as a consummate runner, could smoke and run. However, I suspect he only smoked to relieve pent up tension. With the tankers in sight Bob took back control, got our fuel and with Ubon in the INS and Channel 51 in the TACAN we headed for the barn.

Landing Alive and in One Piece

Landing was uneventful. As we climb out of the aircraft the crew chief cheerfully asked, "How did it go".

"It was a bear" I said.

Bob followed up with, "You'd better check her over real close. They threw a lot of stuff at us today." Arriving at debriefing we both felt like the horse that was "rode hard and put away wet." From their own perspective, each crew described the events of mission to Intel. I asked the officer across the table "we got a 'heads up' that we were under attack moments before any of us saw the MiG. Where did that come from?

"Most likely a College Eye crew," he replied.

"College Eye" I repeated inquisitively.

"Yah, I understand they are old Lockheed Constellations (EC-122D) flown by the 552nd AEW&C Wing out of Korat RTAFB. I think it orbits over water near Haiphong harbor and warns the northern missions about MiGs and potential border incursions."

I then asked "any info on the Weasel crew who bailed out?"

"Sorry, no. I haven't heard anything one way or the other. We are just now putting the pieces together."

I left debriefing with so many thoughts whirling through my head. A hot shower, some food and rest might help, I thought.

My room was dark and cold as I entered. Except for the monotonous hum of the window air conditioner, it was otherwise still – almost too still. It wasn't one of those specific feelings that came over me, but more a disquieting, if not unnerving, premonition. "But a premonition of what?" I thought. Although I couldn't quite put my finger on it, something didn't feel right. John wasn't there but then I assumed he had gone to the club for dinner. Looking around the room I didn't see his flight suit tossed on his bed as was usually the case. No, that wasn't it," I thought. Our cleaning lady had probably taken it off base for washing along with the rest of our laundry. From John's night stand his wife Sharon looked up in my direction from her framed photo. Everything 'looked normal' as I sat down on my bed to remove my flight boots. Everything didn't 'feel normal', however. I dismissed the feeling thinking it would was the events I experienced earlier and would 'go away' after I had a shower, a drink, and some rest.

My Friend was Shot Down

About 30 minutes later I entered the hooch, sat down on an empty bar stool and ordered my usual drink. There wasn't the usual noisy exuberance emanating from the few shadowy figures sitting around in the room. But that didn't seem that unusual as most of the guys were probably at chow. I tuned out my surroundings as my mind drifted aimlessly, focusing on nothing specific, just grateful to be alive. I just stared blankly at the ice cubes in my glass. During this trance the Ops Officer had entered the room and stopped unnoticed behind my stool. It was his hand on my shoulder that brought me instantly back to the moment. He slid onto the stool next to me with a grave expression on his face. As a Lt Colonel pilot, and I a Captain WSO, we weren't on personal terms so his informality and somber expression set off emotional alarm bells. My first thought jumped to home and family. "Had someone died? Had my family been involved in an auto accident or something worse?" In a split second my mind raced through several possible scenarios that might have lead up to him sitting next to me with his hand on my shoulder. About then my mind shifted into slow motion in the same way it had earlier in the day when I came under attack. His hand dropped from my shoulder and face-to-face I said, "What's up, Sir?"

He responded, "Pete, there is no easy way to tell you this --- John and Keith didn't make it back from the morning mission!"

The news was like a slap in the face. I may have let out an inaudible gasp as I tried to assimilate the gravity of his words. He must have seen the stunned disbelief in my expression and waited a second or two for the news to register. He then went on "from the information we have been able to piece together so far, somewhere near Yen Bai, either a SAM or Atoll from a MiG took off the tail of their aircraft. The sky was full of missiles and the other crews didn't see them get hit. All they got was a quick glimpse of their aircraft in flames disappearing through the cloud deck below."

"Did anyone see any chutes", I managed to mutter.

"No one could see chutes because of the cloud deck below," he said "but some in the formation did think they heard a locator beeper."

I am sure I must have replied something to the effect "well at least that's encouraging". Sensing my state of shock he went on to say, "I'll keep you in the loop as we piece more of the events together. Until we learn something to the contrary, John will be listed as MIA (Missing in Action). The Squadron Commander will write

Sharon and the base Chaplin and notification officer back at Seymour will notify her this evening. He will also cut orders for you to act as John's Summary Court's Officer".

"What's that," I replied.

"Well, it means you need to go through and inventory his personal effects, pickup anything he may have ordered from the BX or other merchants, and pay any bills you find". He went on,

"I know you and John were more than roommates. I'll see if I can pull you from tomorrow's mission schedule, but no promises. We are under a lot of pressure to keep the mission count up but I will see what I can do. Keep me informed if you encounter any problems. As an MIA, John's things will have to remain in your room for the next 30 days before you can pack them up for shipment home."

With a slap on my back, he abruptly departed the hooch leaving me still in a state of stunned disbelief. Dozens of thoughts raced through my mind. Had he survived the initial missile explosion? If so, had he been able to eject? Was the parachute beeper someone heard, his or Keith's? If he was alive somewhere in the jungles or rice patties of North Vietnam, would he be able to evade capture?" However, it was virtually impossible for the average American to blend in with the local Asian population. "If or when found, would they capture or shoot him?"

I became aware that the hooch had suddenly seemed to explode with activity and noise as the crews returned from dinner. Apparently, the news of our squadron losing a crew on this morning's mission had spread to the O club. Everyone was trying to gather as much information as possible, culling out fact from fiction. Having lost my apatite I, and many others, would seek memory-numbing solace in the company of Jack Daniels.

Just when I didn't think things could get much worse, someone from our afternoon mission came in with worse news. Although short on specifics it turned out that "no one" had provided the downed Weasel crew "top cover" while they bobbed around in their yellow one- man life rafts. Apparently, the Weasel's wingman returned to his downed buddies after refueling about the same time the Navy rescue boat arrived. All they found was a bullet riddled and deflated life raft floating on the surface of a calm and tranquil sea. Rumors ran the gamut from the crew being executed by AK 47 fire from a North Vietnamese patrol boat out of Haiphong, to them being shot from an enemy helicopter launched from Hainan Island or mainland China.

"If only we had provided 'top cover' for them today", I thought. For a long while I resented the Squadron Commander for his decision. However, over time I came to realize that it is easy to be a Monday morning quarterback when you have all the information -- but not so easy to make such snap decisions with only scraps of information. He was concerned about possibly loosing another plane and crew and probably felt the worse fate the downed fliers might experience would be capture. Wars are full of such split-second decisions, both good and bad, and we just have to deal with their consequences. With the events of the day now becoming blurred by alcohol I headed for the room I knew would be haunted by John's memory. Hopefully I would be able to get some rest before tomorrow and the new mission. Although the Ops Officer said he would try to take me off the schedule, he was either unsuccessful or the promise got lost among more pressing events. There would be another target, another mission, and another day of war awaiting tomorrow's rising sun.

Although all wars are full of specific days its combatants would like to forget, some far worse than that I have just described, for me this day ranked at the top of my long and growing list of bad experiences. Three men unknown to me and probably dead, two more men known to me and who's fate was still to be determined, all lost in a matter of hours. I realize that in other wars, at other times, and under other circumstances, far more victims have died in mere seconds rendering this particular day seemingly insignificant. However, when you are intimately involved in the tragedy of the moment, it is difficult to see it in light of the bigger picture. Did all this contribute to some greater good", I asked myself. This war, and the sacrifices made by both side of the conflict, would continue to go on and on; or so it seemed at the moment. Friends, family and loved ones would continue to grapple with the loss of those who perished all the while trying to find some justification for, or making some sense of, this futile process. Some eventually learn to deal with these tragic moments in life, while others will be haunted by the memories for the rest of their lives. These were two of my "Days Best Forgotten?" What are yours?

Epilogue

From April – October 1972 the Vietnam War was in a state of transition. American ground forces had drawn down to around 6,000 while the air war had accelerated in an attempt to hold the enemy at bay. During this period over 41,000 sorties were flown, many against targets around Hanoi.

Although no authority, I assumed it was hoped the SVN Army would be able to hold their-own while we attempted to negotiate a diplomatic solution. In his famous treatise <u>On War</u>, Carl von Clausewitz once said, "War is a continuation of politics by other means." Vietnam bore witness to this dictum as the politicians and statesman constantly interfered with the implementation of tactics while failing to develop a strategy for success. We would twist the arm of the North Vietnamese to negotiate, while losing men and material, then back off and let them rearm during peace talks. Once the enemy had rearmed and rested, talks would predictably break down and we would resume bombing. The enemy's diplomats "played" our statesmen while Presidents came or quit. In for the 'long haul' the enemy stayed the course while US public opinion, growing war debts and a host of other issues sapped our endurance. Even a movie star played treasonous "footsy" with the enemy appearing in photos sitting on anti-aircraft guns around Hanoi. Our POWs were even tortured when they refused to meet with 'her'.

I left South East Asia days before Christmas 1972. A month later, on 1/27/1973 the US, SVN, ARG, & NVN all signed the Treaty of Paris Accords. Shortly thereafter an official POW list was published. On that list were the names of John and Keith. Missing were the names of the two Weasel crewmen. A few months later John returned home along with hundreds of other prisoners. For the POWs the goal would be to seek peace and try to return to a normal life.

John's pilot Keith, so affected by their ordeal, separated from the AF and entered the ministry.

I suspect that midnight demons will haunt both of them to the end of their lives. For the country, there would be years of sole-searching and social fabric mending. "What did we learn?" one is forced to ask. It has been said that 'those who forget the lessons of history are doomed to repeat them.' Time will tell!

www.ingramcontent.com/pod-product-compliance
Lightning Source LLC
LaVergne TN
LVHW040158080526
838202LV00042B/3218